SPOTLIGHT ON NATURE
ORCA

PAMELA DELL

CREATIVE EDUCATION · CREATIVE PAPERBACKS

Published by Creative Education and Creative Paperbacks
P.O. Box 227, Mankato, Minnesota 56002
Creative Education and Creative Paperbacks are imprints
of The Creative Company
www.thecreativecompany.us

Design and production by Blue Design, Inc.
Art direction by Tom Morgan

Images by Alamy Stock Photo/Calvin W. Hall, 11, David Cook / blueshiftstudios, 2–3, 29, Michael Nolan, 17, WILDLIFE GmbH, 21; Dreamstime/Michael Price, 15, Slowmotiongli, cover; Getty Images/benedek, 26, Gerard Soury, 9, Jeff Foott, 6, Patrick J. Endres, 14; Pexels/Adam Ernster, 29, Pixabay, 28; Shutterstock/Christian Musat, 1; Unsplash/Bart, 10, Lachlan Gowen, 12, Thomas Lipke, 24, Tim Cole, 18, Vidar Nordli-Mathisen, 4–5; Wikimedia Commons/Allen Shimada NOAA/NMFS/OST/AMD, 29, Callan Carpenter, 23, Donald LeRo (NOAA Southwest Fisheries Science Center National Science Foundation), 27, Internet Archive Book Images, 8, 10, 14, 16, 20, 22, m-louis, 16, Robert Pitman, 28, Zaui, 8

Every effort has been made to contact copyright holders for material reproduced in this book. Any omissions will be rectified in subsequent printings if notice is given to the publisher.

Copyright © 2026 Creative Education, Creative Paperbacks
International copyright reserved in all countries. No part of this book may be reproduced in any form without written permission from the publisher.

Library of Congress Cataloging-in-Publication Data
Names: Dell, Pamela author
Title: Orca / by: Pamela Dell.
Description: Mankato, Minnesota : Creative Education and Creative Paperbacks, [2026] | Series: Spotlight on nature | Includes bibliographical references and index. | Audience: Ages 10-13 | Audience: Grades 4-6 | Summary: "An immersive wildlife book for upper-elementary and middle-school readers, featuring a captivating orca pod narrative, stunning photography, and educational tools like infographics, a glossary, and an index. Explores species, habitats, and conservation, making it perfect for nature lovers and young conservationists"-- Provided by publisher.
Identifiers: LCCN 2025017602 (print) | LCCN 2025017603 (ebook) | ISBN 9798895810798 library binding | ISBN 9798896800323 paperback | ISBN 9798895812051 ebook
Subjects: LCSH: Killer whale--Juvenile literature
Classification: LCC QL737.C432 D46 2026 (print) | LCC QL737.C432 (ebook) | DDC 599.53/6--dc23/eng/20250813
LC record available at https://lccn.loc.gov/2025017602
LC ebook record available at https://lccn.loc.gov/2025017603

Printed in the United States

CONTENTS

MEET THE FAMILY   4
Orcas of the Northeast Pacific

LIFE BEGINS   7
FEATURED FAMILY
Welcome to the Family
First Meal   10

EARLY ADVENTURES   13
FEATURED FAMILY
Young and Dependent   14
Give It a Try   16

LIFE LESSONS   19
FEATURED FAMILY
This Is How It's Done   20
Practice Makes Perfect   22

HELPING ORCAS SURVIVE   25

Family Album Snapshots   28
Words to Know   30
Learn More   31
Index   32

MEET THE FAMILY
Orcas of the Northeast Pacific

The vast Northern Pacific Ocean stretches east from Japan to the western shores of Canada and Alaska and Washington in the United States. Sea grasses cling to rocks and sway in the chilly waters along the rugged coastline. Sea urchins, snails, and many fish **species** hide in towering underwater kelp forests. Seals, whales, and other mammals live there too. One striking mammal found in these waters is the sleek, black-and-white orca. The northeastern Pacific is home to two main orca groups. These are the Northern Resident and the Southern Resident communities.

In shallow waters off the coast of northern Vancouver Island, Canada, a Northern Resident orca has grown sluggish. She has little appetite. This orca is at the end of her 17-month pregnancy. Finally, her baby is born. As soon as it exits its mother's body, the baby is urged to the water's surface. Its first life-giving breath is top priority.

CLOSE-UP
Blowhole
An orca breathes through a blowhole on its head, opening it by contracting muscles and closing it by relaxing them.

CHAPTER ONE
LIFE BEGINS

Long ago, sailors called orcas "whale killers" because of their aggressive hunting skills. Eventually, those two words got reversed. Today orcas are also known as killer whales. But they are not whales. Orcas are the largest members of the dolphin family

Orcas are **apex predators**, found in all the world's oceans. Despite being a single species, orcas can be divided into at least ten different ecotypes. The members of each **ecotype** share characteristics based on the ecotype's geographical location. These include variances in size, markings, diet, and social habits.

Orcas are one of the most recognizable marine mammals on earth. They are mostly black on top with a white patch behind the eyes and mostly white undersides. Of all the ecotypes, most is known about the orcas of the northeastern Pacific. These adult males weigh up to about 13,300 pounds (6,000 kilograms). Their length may reach 27 feet (8.2 meters). Female

ORCA MILESTONES

DAY 1

- White body areas appear peach-colored
- Weight: 265 to 353 pounds (120 to 160 kg)
- Length: 8.5 feet (2.6 m)
- Nurses for 5 to 10 seconds several times per hour

orcas weigh roughly half of what males do and grow to about 23 feet (7 m).

All orcas are highly social, extremely intelligent animals. They belong to large groups called clans. Clans are divided into closely knit smaller groups called pods. A pod may have only a few members or as many as 30 or more. Members of the same pod are all related through their mothers, or their matriline. Mothers and their children remain together throughout their entire lives. A pod travels together led by its older females.

Communication is a crucial skill for orcas because they travel great distances. Every pod has its own unique **dialect**, or collection of calls. They use these calls to "talk" to each

CLOSE-UP
Flukes

An orca's tail has two flukes made of tough, boneless tissue. Back muscles control their up-and-down movement.

——————— FEATURED FAMILY ———————

Welcome to the World

The Northern Resident orca calf comes into the world tail first. She weighs somewhere around 350 to 400 pounds (159 to 181 kilograms). Her birth takes about one to two hours. Inside the womb, her fins and tail flukes were floppy. Being born tail first gives these essential swimming tools a chance to gradually harden in the cold water. Some pod females may stay close during the birth. They ward off potentially aggressive males. The calf's mother or an "auntie" will guide her quickly to the water's surface. With her first breaths, life truly begins.

other. Orcas also make clicks and whistling sounds for **echolocation** and other purposes. Young orcas exhibit a form of "babbling" as they learn to communicate with their pod.

Orcas are strictly meat eaters. Their diet depends on where they live. They may eat fish, seabirds, or marine mammals such as seals and sharks. Baby orcas, called calves, start out just nursing on their mother's milk. Mothers get much help from other pod members in raising their calves. But calves stay close to their mothers to nurse and learn. Calves won't taste meat until they're at least a year old.

1 WEEK
▸ Nurses about 45 minutes total per day

3 WEEKS
▸ Nurses 10 minutes or less per day

CLOSE-UP
Countershading

In choppy water, an orca is hard to spot due to countershading—its dark back blends with the depths, and its pale belly matches the sunlit surface.

––––––––––––––– FEATURED FAMILY –––––––––––––––

First Meal

The newborn calf has begun breathing. Now it is time to eat. Her mother takes a horizontal position in shallow water. She arches her tail. Swimming on its side, the calf finds one of her mother's two nipples. But learning to nurse successfully is a bit of a challenge. It may take up to several hours before the calf gets a good taste of her mother's rich milk. As she begins to learn, she takes short drinks of about 15 to 20 seconds each, many times each hour. Mealtime gradually improves.

A POD
of orcas may have dozens of related members.

2 MONTHS
- Nurses 5 minutes or less per day

11 WEEKS
- Teeth are growing in

CLOSE-UP
Melon

The melon, a fatty tissue in orcas' foreheads, channels their high-frequency clicks into the water for communication and echolocation.

CHAPTER TWO
EARLY ADVENTURES

The mother orca has a demanding job. She must teach, discipline, and feed a young calf as well as herself. All orcas form strong social bonds within their pods. So females also support their older children and other pod members. They may provide food or protection from danger.

When a calf is first born, the white areas of its body have a light peachy color. Researchers believe this is caused by blood vessels showing through before the calf has developed more **blubber**. These parts whiten as the calf gains weight and fat over time. Newborns also have whiskers which fall off soon after birth.

An orca calf naturally knows how to swim at birth. But its mother stays near. She watches her calf closely, directing its movements. As the pod travels, calves follow along, usually swimming in their mothers' wake. This position is less tiring for the calves, whose muscle strength is just developing.

① YEAR
- Has grown about 25 additional inches (64 cm)
- Has gained about 882 pounds (400 kg)

CLOSE-UP
Blubber

Under an orca's skin is a 3- to 4-inch (7.6–10 cm) layer of fat called blubber. Blubber stores energy and helps retain heat.

 FEATURED FAMILY

Young and Dependent

For the first month of her life, the Northern Resident calf has fed only on her mother's milk. She has also had no sleep at all. Neither has her mother. Both stay awake constantly as the mother keeps a watch out for sharks and makes sure her calf knows how to breathe. When the calf finally starts sleeping, half of her brain stays awake so she can take occasional breaths. As with all orcas, the calf must make a conscious effort to breathe. She will suffocate if her brain goes to sleep.

Young calves grow more curious and playful as they grow. They may play with objects found in the water as well as with each other. Sometimes calves form attachments, or "friendships," with other young orcas in their pod. These pals hang out and play together. Playing means head-butting and vigorously slapping their tails against the water. They may even snap their jaws, bite, and scrape their teeth across the other's bodies, called raking. All of this is practice for adult life. It also helps figure out who's the most dominant in the pod, aside from the oldest females.

(2) YEARS

- Has grown about 21 additional inches (53 cm)
- Teeth fully grown in
- Has stopped feeding on mother's milk

EARLY ADVENTURES

CLOSE-UP
Teeth

Orcas have strong, cone-shaped teeth and a powerful bite for hunting. They don't chew—just rip prey into chunks. Lost teeth don't grow back.

—— FEATURED  FAMILY ——

Give It a Try

At a year old, the calf's teeth are growing in sharp and pointed. Her peachy patches are gradually turning white. Lively and playful, she is becoming more independent. She is so energetic she sometimes breaches the water's surface 18 times in a row. The calf has not yet participated in active hunting. But she is finally starting to try solid food. Her mother gives her chunks of salmon, her pod's favorite fish. If her mother is busy, her grandmother or another female relative feeds her.

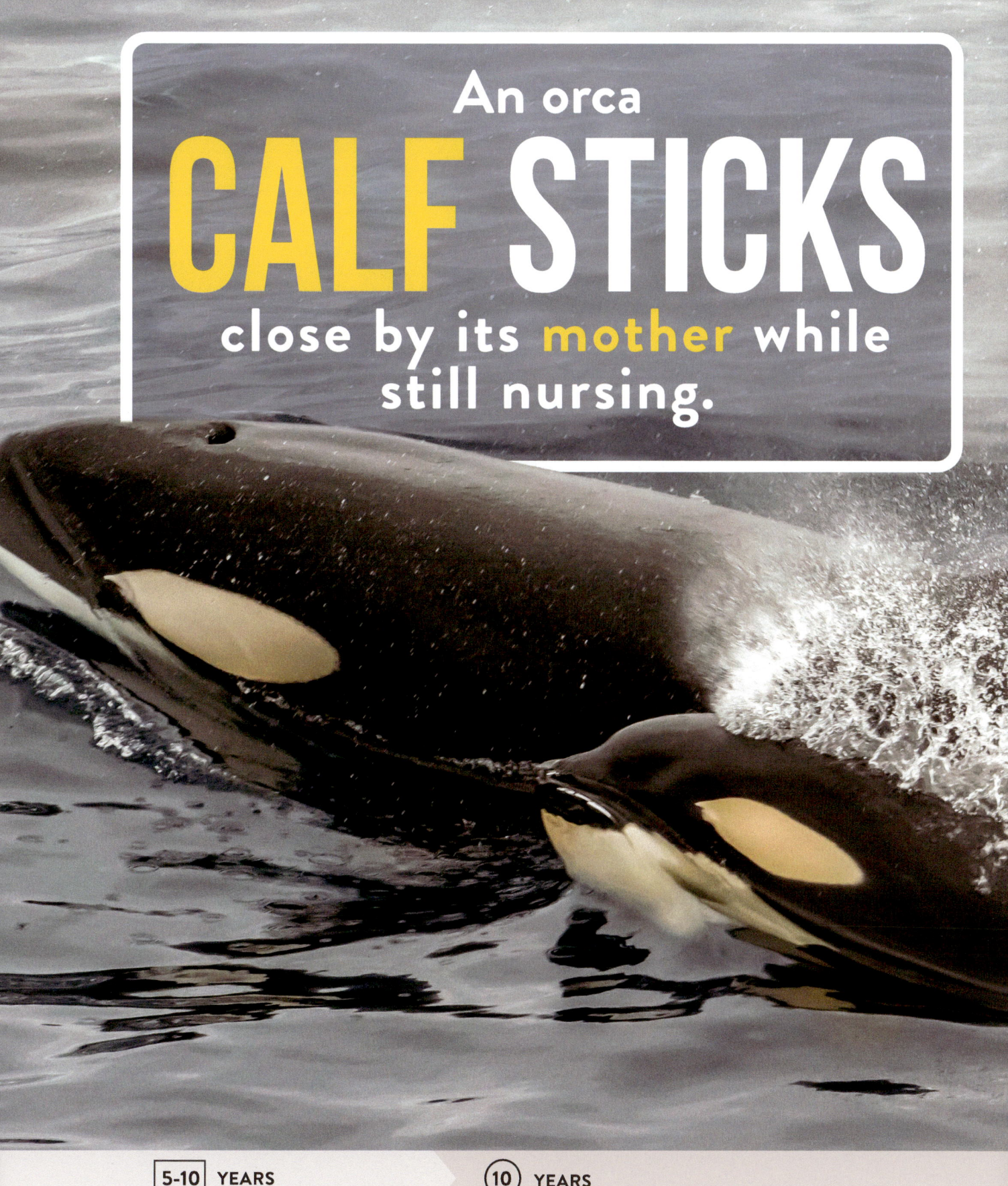

An orca **CALF STICKS** close by its **mother** while still nursing.

5-10 YEARS	10 YEARS
▸ No longer a calf, transitioning to adulthood	▸ Females have become sexually mature

EARLY ADVENTURES

CLOSE-UP
Saddle Patch

Orcas have a saddle patch behind their dorsal fin. Individual orcas have distinct saddles, making identification easier.

CHAPTER THREE
LIFE LESSONS

Male orcas are the "mama's boys" of the marine mammal world. They venture out mainly to mate with females from other pods. But they have no fathering role. Instead, they return to their mother's pod. This is their community for life.

Back "at home," male orcas continue to rely on their mothers. A mother orca will often catch prey to feed to her son, even when he is an adult. Adult females don't get this kind of pampering. They remain busy, hunting and caring for their young and others in the pod.

Orcas ordinarily are observed only at the water's surface. This makes it difficult to know much about them. Only the Northern and Southern Resident populations have been extensively studied. But all orcas form strong social bonds. They spend their days swimming, resting, hunting, and playing together. They rest at night.

(13) YEARS
- Males have become sexually mature

(4) YEARS
- Teeth showing wear
- Females begin reproducing
- Females stop taking food from mothers

Pod members stay in constant communication while traveling, even when widely spread out. If a sick or injured orca can't reach the surface to breathe, other orcas in its pod lift it up to help. Orcas have also saved humans from drowning in this same way.

Mothers show their young what food to eat and how to hunt for it. Calves also learn their ecotype's dialect and their pod's "correct" social behaviors. But life in the waters can be rough. Only about 50 percent or fewer make it to a year old. If they survive into adulthood, males typically live around 30 to 50 years. Females live longer, sometimes as long as 80 or 90 years.

CLOSE-UP
Dorsal Fin

The triangular dorsal fin projects upward from an orca's back, helping provide stability in the water. Every orca's fin is unique, but males have the largest of any marine mammal, sometimes reaching 6 feet (1.8 m) tall. Female dorsal fins are shorter and curve backwards.

— FEATURED FAMILY —

This Is How It's Done

The Northern Resident calf is just past her second birthday. She has recently stopped nursing. Now she mainly eats fish, picking up skills as she swims with the pod. She also has a new "best friend," another young female, about three years old. When the pod travels, these two swim close together. They communicate with whistles and clicks. They rub noses and share slippery hugs, showing their close relationship. When the pod corrals a frantic school of fish, the older orcas quickly catch prey. The younger orcas are slower, but everybody eats.

40 YEARS

▸ Females stop reproducing

LIFE LESSONS

The pod provides adolescent orcas with security as they learn. Along with these skills, they stop "babbling." Now they understand their pod's language and can truly communicate. Young orcas also observe and then practice the pod's group hunting tactics. These might include bouncing a seal off an ice floe or flipping a shark on its back. All hunting techniques are passed down within each individual ecotype. Young orcas eventually master their pod's specific hunting methods. Now they're ready to contribute real value to the pod.

— FEATURED FAMILY —

Practice Makes Perfect

Within her pod, the four-year-old orca has learned a lot. Her mother has another calf on the way. But until that birth, the young orca is still the baby of her family, if not the pod's youngest. Her mother still offers her food, even though her calf has become a skilled hunter. The pod hunts in a "wolf pack." Their movements are cooperative and well-coordinated as they go after some tasty Chinook salmon. With her speed and powerful bite, the young orca scores a 25-pounder (11 kg). It's her well-deserved prize, but she generously shares.

Orcas create powerful waves that knock **seals** off ice and into the water.

50-60 YEARS	80-90 YEARS
▸ Teeth heavily worn ▸ End of life for males	▸ End of life for females

CHAPTER FOUR
HELPING ORCAS SURVIVE

The world's orcas, or killer whales, need to be protected and preserved. But these animals are more wide-ranging than any other **cetacean**. That makes it difficult to count them. In 2023, researchers estimated the total orca population to be only about 50,000. Despite being the oceans' most cunning predators, orcas face many dangers. Unfortunately, humans are usually the primary threat.

Orcas get entangled in old fishing nets and other equipment carelessly tossed overboard. Some sustain serious injury and may even die. Other hazards include being hit by boats or their propellers.

Pollutants like plastics, oil spills, chemicals, and sewage are a major threat to orcas. These toxins weaken them and slow their recovery from illness and injury. Another form of pollution is underwater noise. Orcas navigate their world by echolocation and their sense of hearing. Communicating and hunting are critical to their survival. Yet noise from boat traffic, underwater construction, and other sources reduces both of

CLOSE-UP
Pectoral Fins
An orca's rounded pectoral fins (flippers) help it steer and stop. Inside the flippers are bones with five digits, like human fingers.

these survival skills, causing stress. A simple lack of food is also a serious problem for some ecotypes.

A few orca subpopulations are the verge of **extinction**. The so-called West Coast Community that inhabits coastal areas in the United Kingdom is down to fewer than ten orcas. The Southern Resident population of the eastern North Pacific has under 100. A group in the Strait of Gibraltar is listed as critically endangered.

Numerous organizations are dedicated to protecting the world's orcas. Orca Conservancy in Washington state and ORCA in the United Kingdom are only two of these. Some are working to increase prey stock in areas where orcas are running out of food. Others focus on saving vital habitat and setting up protective laws. Most welcome volunteers in different capacities.

There is also a vast worldwide push to end the capture of orcas for human entertainment. Capturing orcas is a violent and dangerous activity. It drastically disrupts pod communities. Much data proves that keeping orcas in confined spaces harms them.

Even small efforts can help the world's orcas. Recycle plastics. Report orca sightings. "Adopt" an orca through donations. All of this furthers the global movement to keep these beautiful and majestic creatures thriving.

FAMILY ALBUM
SNAPSHOTS

The orca's Latin species name is Orcinus Orca. The English translation of "Orcinus" is kingdom of the dead.

Orcas belong to the sub-order of toothed whales.

Behavioral studies indicate that orcas are the most curious and playful of all cetaceans.

During a pregnancy that lasts 15 to 18 months, a mother orca will put on 500 to 600 pounds (227 to 272 kilograms).

Orcas stop reproducing in their forties. Then they take on a kind of "grandmother" role. This sometimes includes "babysitting."

Drone footage shows that young resident orcas prefer to socialize with others about their same age and of their own gender.

At birth, Northern Pacific orca calves are assigned a number according to the pod they belong to. Each also gets a nickname, such as Current or Saddle.

Northern Resident orcas love to visit "rubbing beaches." Here they com very close to shore where they can rub their bodies against the pebbles there.

The first-ever orca to perform for humans, a Northern Resident named Namu, was caught in 1965. He died after less than a year in captivity.

Southern Resident orcas are critically endangered due to being hunted for captivity in the mid-1900s. Today, the salmon they eat is also running out.

Up to 69 percent of Southern Resident orca pregnancies fail or the calves die shortly after birth. The area's lack of salmon is the main cause.

SNAPSHOTS

WORDS to Know

apex predators   animals at the top of the food chain; animals that hunt and are not usually hunted by other animals

blubber   fatty tissue found in sea mammals such as dolphins, whales, and seals

breaching   the act of rising up and breaking the water's surface by a marine mammal

cetecean   A kind of ocean animal that includes whales, dolphins, and porpoises.

dialect   a unique form of language used by a specific social group or inhabitants of a specific location

echolocation   the skill of some animals to locate objects by sending out sound waves and listening for the echoes that bounce back

ecotype   animals that belong to the same species but which have different characteristics according to the environment they live in

extinct   no longer in existence

species   a group of living things that have shared characteristics and that are able to reproduce with one another

LEARN MORE

Books

Krajnik, Elizabeth. *Orcas (Killers of the Animal World series)*. New York, NY: Rosen Publishing, 2020.

Mann, Dionna. *Orcas (Nature's Children Series)*. New York, NY: Children's Press/Scholastic, 2019.

Sandstrom, Donna. *Orca Rescue! The True Story of an Orphaned Orca Called Springer*. Toronto, Ont., Canada: Kids Can Press, 2021.

Websites

"Orca" National Geographic Kids.

https://kids.nationalgeographic.com/animals/mammals/facts/orca

"Killer Whale Facts!" National Geographic Kids.

https://www.natgeokids.com/uk/discover/animals/sea-life/killer-whale-facts/

"Killer Whale." Britannica Kids.

https://kids.britannica.com/students/article/killer-whale/576927

Documentaries

Barthod, Jean-François [director]. "A Man Among Orcas." St. Thomas Productions, Available on YouTube (https://www.youtube.com/watch?v1uW9mcGordLY)

Chavez, Raymond and Minasian, Stanley M. [writers/producers]. "The Free Willy Story: Keiko's Journey Home." Available on YouTube and Prime Video.

(https://www.youtube.com/watch?v1p6lpm4zKo2E)

Note: Every effort has been made to ensure that any websites listed above were active at the time of publication. However, because of the nature of the Internet, it is impossible to guarantee that these sites will remain active indefinitely or that their contents will not be altered.

Visit

CHANNEL ISLANDS NATIONAL PARK

Experience orca sightings by joining a whale-watching cruise from Oxnard Harbor, where the pristine waters surrounding the islands attract marine life
4151 Victoria Avenue, Oxnard, CA 93035

GLACIER BAY NATIONAL PARK

Embark on a boat tour through Glacier Bay's nutrient-rich inlets and glacial fjords for a chance to observe orcas in their natural habitat.
Glacier Bay National Park & Preserve, PO Box 140, Gustavus, AK 99826

KENAI FJORDS NATIONAL PARK

Opt for a guided boat excursion departing from Seward to witness orcas alongside dramatic fjords and coastal scenery in this rugged marine park.
Kenai Fjords National Park Visitor Center, 1212 4th Avenue, Seward, AK 99664

INDEX

apex predator, 7
calf development 9, 13, 15, 17, 20, 22
communication, 8, 12, 19
cooperative behavior, 15, 22, 23
diet, 7, 9
echolocation, 9, 12, 25
ecotype dialect
group hunting, 22
lifespan, 20

maternal dependence, 19
morphological features, 6, 8, 20, 26
northeastern Pacific, 4, 7
northern resident, 4, 8, 14, 20, 29
pod structure 8, 9, 11, 13, 19, 22
rescue behavior, 20
social learning, 8, 13, 20